# BLIZZARDS

**Steven Otfinoski**

TFCB

# TWENTY-FIRST CENTURY BOOKS

**A Division of Henry Holt and Company**
**New York**

Twenty-First Century Books
A division of Henry Holt and Company, Inc.
115 West 18th Street
New York, New York 10011

Henry Holt® and colophon are trademarks of Henry Holt and
Company, Inc.
*Publishers since 1866*

Published in Canada by Fitzhenry & Whiteside Ltd.
195 Allstate Parkway, Markham, Ontario L3R 4T8

Printed in the United States of America

All editions are printed on acid-free paper ∞.

Created and produced in association with Blackbirch Graphics, Inc.

**Library of Congress Cataloging-in-Publication Data**

Otfinoski, Steve.
  Blizzards / Steve Otfinoski. — 1st ed.
       p.     cm. — (When disaster strikes)
  Includes index.
  ISBN 0-8050-3093-X
  1. Blizzards—North America—Juvenile literature. 2. Snow removal—North
America—Juvenile literature. [1. Blizzards.] I. Title. II. Series.
QC926.37.O84    1994
363.3'49—dc20                                                    93-38522
                                                                    CIP
                                                                    AC

# Contents

**1.** *Snow and More Snow*     *5*

**2.** *Blizzard Country*     *17*

**3.** *Eastern Blizzards*     *29*

**4.** *Blizzard Preparation and Protection*     *47*

*Glossary*     *59*

*Further Reading*     *61*

*Have You Ever Faced a Disaster?*     *62*

*Source Notes*     *62*

*Index*     *63*

# Snow and More Snow

Many weather forecasters called it The Storm of the Century. They weren't exaggerating. In mid-March of 1993, a winter storm whirled up from the Gulf of Mexico, first striking Florida, and then the rest of the Eastern Seaboard. The snow it brought was only part of the storm's danger. Tornadoes that sprang out of the massive blizzard killed many people. Some areas in the normally warm southern states of Alabama, Georgia, and Tennessee saw as much as 2 feet (0.5 meters) of snow, and snowdrifts that were 6 feet (2 meters) high.

*Opposite*:
Atlanta, Georgia, was blanketed with snow in March 1993.

"I'm six-foot-five," Jeff Higgenbotham of Dalton, Georgia, told one reporter, "and I went outside a little while ago and was up to my knees in snow. It's a pretty sight...but I'd rather have somebody send me a postcard of it than be in it."

By the time the storm ended on March 14, the entire Eastern Seaboard north to Quebec, Canada, had experienced the worst blizzard of the twentieth century. It was described by one weather forecaster as "a hurricane with snow."

## What Is a Blizzard?

Blizzard—the very word sends a chill down the spine and brings to mind blinding snow and frigid temperatures. But just what makes a blizzard different from any other snowstorm? There are three main components to a blizzard—very cold temperatures, heavy snow, and most important of all, wind. Strong winds are what gives a blizzard its tremendous power. Wind can drive snow so hard that visibility can be reduced to zero. It can sweep snow into monstrous drifts that can bury a car, or even an entire building.

The National Weather Service in Washington, D.C., defines a blizzard as any snowfall that is accompanied by sustained winds of 35 miles (56 kilometers) per hour or more, temperatures that fall as low as 10°F (-12°C), and visibility of less than 1,500 feet (458 meters). These conditions, the Weather Service reports, must persist for at least three hours to cause a snowstorm to turn into a blizzard. A severe blizzard has winds that are greater than 45 miles (72 kilometers) per hour, temperatures below 10°F (-12°C), and visibility approaching zero.

## HOW A FRONT FORMS

The place where warm air and cold air meet is called a front. As cool air, which is heavier, moves forward, it slides under warm air, which is lighter. The warm air is pushed up, and as it rises, it is cooled. The cool air can hold less moisture and precipitation begins.

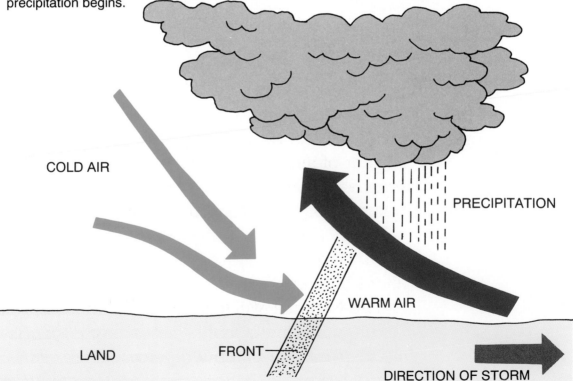

COLD AIR

PRECIPITATION

WARM AIR

LAND

FRONT

DIRECTION OF STORM

Where do such powerful snowstorms come from? Oddly enough, many blizzards develop after a period of very warm weather, often in late winter. A cold air mass from the Arctic region heads south into the more temperate zone, where the air is warmer. The cold, heavy air causes warm, moist air to rise between the two air masses. The boundary formed by this rising air is called a cold front. The rising air causes clouds of water vapor to form ice crystals that we call snow. It also produces the cold, northerly winds that drive the snow.

Central Canada and the midwestern section of the United States get the most blizzards, although blizzards are common in the Northeast and have also been known to strike the South, Southwest, and West. Blizzards can occur from September through May, but in the Northern Hemisphere, most of them strike during the four coldest months of the year—December, January, February, and March. As many as 35 blizzards have occurred throughout the United States in one year.

## The Dangers of Blizzards

A quiet snowfall can be one of winter's greatest pleasures. Falling snow is fun to watch and fun to play in. But a blizzard is another story. It is a serious disaster that can be life-threatening. A

# THE MAN WHO CAPTURED SNOWFLAKES

Snow, the main ingredient in any blizzard, is still largely a mysterious substance to scientists. The icy crystals called snowflakes have fascinated humans since early times, but it was only a little more than a hundred years ago that someone first photographed them and actually conducted a scientific study.

Mr. Wilson ("Snowflake") Bentley was born on a small farm in Jericho, Vermont, on February 9, 1865. His mother first sparked his interest in snow by showing him snowflakes under a microscope that the family had. The incredible diversity of shapes and the intricate structure of each flake fascinated Bentley, and soon he was trying to draw snowflakes to preserve their images. Bentley's efforts were frustrated, however, because the flakes would melt before he could sketch

them. One day his father bought him a simple camera and Bentley built an enlarger in order to photograph the snowflakes clearly. Bentley would capture snowflakes as they fell, place them on glass slides, and photograph them through the microscope.

For fifty years, Bentley studied snowflakes. He discovered that no two flakes were exactly alike, but that they all fell into several categories. He called three of these categories stellar crystals, copper columns, and ice needles. In 1931, the year Bentley died, more than 3,000 of his photographs were published in a book titled *Snow Crystals*. His pioneering work on snowflakes encouraged others to study them, increasing our knowledge of both snowflakes and the storms that create them.

person caught outdoors in a blizzard can easily lose all sense of direction in the blinding snow. People have been known to get lost within a few yards of their homes and freeze to death in blizzards. The heavy snowfall from a blizzard can cause roofs to collapse, trapping and even killing the people below. Also, poor visibility and icy or snowbound roads may make driving hazardous and can lead to many automobile accidents.

Blizzards are life-threatening in other ways, too. Some people perish in fires caused by overloaded heating systems or the improper use of alternative heating systems, such as gas or kerosene heaters. Others, trapped in their cars, die from breathing poisonous fumes given off by car exhaust when they keep the motor running to stay warm. Still other people, especially the elderly, suffer from heart attacks and strokes while shoveling the snow that a blizzard leaves in its wake.

Animals can also die in blizzards. Cattle, sheep, and other livestock can freeze or starve to death in pastures and unheated barns.

But the destruction often goes beyond the loss of human and animal life. Farmers can lose entire crops as well. A blizzard that strikes the normally warm southern states can have a negative effect on the growing season. During

A snowstorm in 1948 caused 173 telephone poles to crash down onto a state highway in Illinois, cutting off all communication to several areas.

some winter storms, citrus growers in Florida have burned smudge pots (fuel-burning containers used to protect trees from frost) and old tires in an attempt to save their fruit trees. Despite their efforts, many growers still sustained heavy financial losses when their orange and grapefruit crops were destroyed by the severe ice and cold from winter storms.

Agricultural areas are not the only ones devastated by blizzards. In large industrial cities, life is often brought to a standstill. A blizzard's tremendous winds may knock down power and telephone lines, causing vast power outages and a loss of communications. Traffic slows to a halt on snowbound roads and streets, and stores run out of foodstuffs because delivery trucks can't get through. Airports, railroads, and highways shut down because it is too dangerous to travel, leaving thousands stranded.

While many people don't mind staying at home and can manage to do so during a blizzard, others must get out. Firefighters, special medical teams, police officers, and other professionals need to get to the scene of emergencies to help. If the snow stops them, the results are often tragic.

For all their destructiveness, blizzards are not completely bad. Much of the land in the western part of the United States is arid (very dry). People who live in this part of the country depend on heavy snows to provide their water supply. Snow that is deposited in the high mountains melts in the spring and runs down into reservoirs that have been constructed specifically to hold this water. The water is then used for both irrigation and drinking water throughout the year.

Anyone who lives in Colorado or Vermont knows that the snow blizzards bring is a very important part of the local economy. Resorts in places such as Stowe, Vermont, Vail and Aspen, Colorado, and Squaw Valley, California, offer skiing and other winter sports that attract tourists. These tourists, in turn, generate a considerable amount of income.

Winter snows in Squaw Valley, California, help the local economy by drawing tourists to the area.

*Opposite:*
Without heavy snows, it would not be possible to enjoy winter activities such as skiing, snowmobiling, and sledding.

Winter snows have other benefits in addition to helping provide tourist attractions, and supplying water in the western United States. When winter snow melts, it provides the moisture that is necessary for grain to grow in the Northern Plains. Without this water, crops would not get the amount of water needed to thrive. Blizzards help this region live up to its reputation as "America's breadbasket."

△ **15**

# *Blizzard Country*

There is a section of North America where more blizzards occur than in any other part of the continent. Often referred to as blizzard country, this region includes the midwestern United States, as well as central Canada.

Blizzard conditions are a way of life in this area. People have adapted their lives to deal with the dangers and inconveniences of snowstorms. They build homes with steeped roofs to prevent snow from piling up on them. Some experts estimate that about 50 pounds (23 kilograms) of snow can pile up on every square foot (square meter) of a flat roof, often causing it to cave in. Snow fences are erected along fields that line the roadways to prevent driving

*Opposite:*
South Dakota is in the heart of blizzard country.

blizzard winds from hurling snow into tall drifts on the roads. The drifts build up along the snow fences, instead.

Farmers plan ahead for the snow, too. They plant their wheat in the fall. It lies under the protective cover of snow all winter and then sprouts above the earth in the spring, watered by the melting snow.

Getting around in blizzard country after a bad storm isn't hard when you know how. In rural parts of Canada, people wear snowshoes, which resemble tennis racquets with a wide webbing of strings. The webbing prevents the wearer's feet from sinking into deep snow. To travel great distances, people in blizzard country use dogsleds, snowmobiles, and small automobiles that have skilike runners in front instead of wheels. The rear wheels of these vehicles are big tractor tires. Snowmobiles can go nearly anyplace a dogsled can. Ski planes, which can land on snow and frozen lakes, are an even more versatile way of traveling. They are ideal for people who must travel long distances in blizzard country. "Bush pilots" hire out their small planes and make a living transporting people from place to place.

Despite their ability to cope with the problems brought by severe snowstorms, the people of blizzard country have not been unaffected by

Snowmobiles are a fun and efficient solution to the tricky problem of getting around in blizzard country.

these disastrous storms. Some of the many blizzards that have hit this area have been among the most destructive storms in North American history.

## Snowstorms of the Blizzard State

South Dakota has had some of the worst blizzards in U.S. history. This has earned it the nickname the "blizzard state." South Dakota had a terrible winter during 1880–1881. Blizzard

# THE DONNER PARTY TRAGEDY

A great tragedy in American history was caused by blizzards during the winter of 1846-1847. In April of 1846, a group of 87 pioneers—men, women, and children—from Illinois and nearby states set out for California across the Sierra Nevada Mountains. Led by George and Jacob Donner, they arrived at the High Sierras on October 31, only to find the mountain pass was blocked by heavy snow. Unable to continue their journey until spring, the pioneers built crude cabins to protect them from the blinding blizzards that regularly swept through the pass.

"The storm blows so thick and fast that we cannot see twenty feet [six meters] looking against the wind," wrote J.F. Reed in his diary. "I dread the coming night....It is still snowing and very cold."

When their food supply ran out, the Donner Party prepared to slaughter their oxen, but the beasts had wandered off in the swirling snows and were lost. The pioneers then ate mice and twigs to survive. The Reed family also ate their family dog, Cash. According to 13-year-old Virginia Reed, they ate "his head and feet and hide and everything about him. We lived on little Cash a week." Then, as some of the pioneers died from starvation and illness, a number of the survivors ate their flesh to stay alive.

The first of four relief parties arrived with packs of food in February 1847. When one woman stepped out of her cabin and saw them, she cried, "Are you from California or Heaven?" Other survivors were too numb from suffering to react with any enthusiasm. One wrote in a diary: "Froze hard last night; 7 men arrived from California yesterday evening with provisions." Of the original members of the Donner party, only 47 survived the storm.

Today, the snow-blocked mountain pass that brought death to 40 adventurous settlers is called Donner Pass.

snow started falling in October and continued off and on right into spring. When the snows finally melted, there was extensive flooding throughout the state. An ice dam backed up ice and water for 30 miles (48 kilometers) on the Missouri River. When the dam broke, the waters flooded and destroyed an entire village. Steamboats at the docks were crushed, and a church floated downstream, its bells ringing loudly.

The Blizzard of 1888 (January 12–14) in South Dakota was less fierce, but far deadlier, than the blizzards of 1880–1881 because the state's population had increased considerably in just a few years. Winds gusting to 60 miles (97 kilometers) per hour drove snow into people's faces like tiny bullets and knocked over grain elevators, scattering tons of stored grains across the land. Passengers on trains that were crossing the prairie were trapped in them for up to three days. In all, 174 South Dakotans died in this storm.

The Blizzard of 1905 was less destructive to people. However, it killed thousands of cattle that were grazing on open ranges in the western part of the state. Almost overnight, many cattlemen were financially ruined by this terrible winter storm.

South Dakota's more recent blizzards have not been as destructive as some of the earlier ones, but blizzards still continue to hit the state just as often as they did in the past. Two or three severe winter storms can be expected to occur somewhere in the blizzard state nearly every winter.

This house in Denver, Colorado, was completely buried during the 1949 blizzard. Neighbors helped the owners dig out their house once the storm died down.

## The "Great White Death": 1949

The Great Blizzard of 1949 was one of the most devastating storm systems to ever hit blizzard country. It was actually a series of blizzards that lasted seven long weeks from January 2 to February 19. The first blizzard struck Wyoming and Colorado, paralyzing many towns and cities within an hour. It soon spread out over most of the West, from Nevada to the Northern Plains. Snowdrifts up to 30 feet (9 meters) high were reported. The storm stranded hundreds of people who could only be rescued by airplane. These snowbound people let the pilots know what kind of help they needed by making marks in the snow. A straight line meant that a doctor was needed, while an "F" meant that food supplies were running short.

Operation Snowbound helped hundreds of people survive The Blizzard of 1949. Here, a vehicle from the 215th Air Rescue Unit drags a sled load of supplies to a snowbound ranch in Nebraska.

However, even the rescuers themselves were in danger. One pilot smashed his aircraft into a mountainside. He was stranded in the snow for

six days, his feet frozen, before another pilot came to his aid. Other people weren't as lucky. A family in Rockport, Colorado, left their snowbound car to cross an open prairie in order to reach their house. They were later found frozen to death in a field close to their home.

To open snow-clogged roads, the U.S. Army started Operation Snowbound. The troops, under the direction of General Lewis A. Pick, opened up more than 100,000 miles (161,000 kilometers) of highway in 40 days with bulldozers, road graders, and snowplows. In order to save millions of cattle and sheep in Nebraska, South Dakota, and other states, the U.S. Air Force dropped 1,500 tons (1,361 metric tons) of hay from 80 aircraft. They also dropped 1,000 tons (907 metric tons) of flour and 12 tons (11 metric tons) of alfalfa pellets. "We've dropped everything the people have asked for, whether it's to a small farm or ranch or a snowbound village," Colonel Joe McNay, in charge of operations at Offutt Air Base, near Omaha, told a reporter. "Why, the other day we even dropped a half ounce of radium that was worth $500,000. A hospital in western Nebraska needed it badly.

"We've also evacuated nearly 300 expectant mothers from villages and ranches. We've been keeping pretty busy," he added. Despite these heroic efforts, more than 100 people and nearly

1 million head of livestock perished in what one reporter called the "Great White Death."

## *The Blizzards of 1966*

Another major blizzard in March 1966 was more localized than the storm of 1949, but it was just as brutal. On March 3, a blizzard stalled over the Dakotas for fifteen hours. The late winter storm caught many people by surprise. Three basketball coaches were trapped in a car for nearly four days near Mandan, North Dakota. To keep warm, they cracked open the windows for air and built a fire inside the car. A farmer and his family stranded in another car survived for several days on fifteen candy bars, the only food they had with them. Among the 18 people who died in the blizzard was a 12-year-old girl who was trying to shut the door of the family chicken house only 100 feet (31 meters) away from her house. Tragically, she was found frozen to death the next day.

Another blizzard struck on March 21, 1966, bringing more destruction, to Iowa, Nebraska, Minnesota, and Michigan. Lightning and rains preceded the storm, which dropped 9 inches (23 centimeters) of snow on the area. Although this was not an unusual amount of snowfall, the heavy wetness of the snow made it cling to whatever it touched. Trees and telephone poles

sagged and broke, and power lines snapped. Icicles stuck straight out from house eaves, parallel to the ground, formed by the powerful force of the wind. Twenty-seven people, throughout these states, lost their lives before the storm ended.

## The Blizzards of 1981–1982

As in 1966, a series of terrible blizzards struck the Midwest during the winter of 1981-1982. The first storm hit the Twin Cities of Minneapolis and St. Paul in Minnesota in November 1981, dumping 14 inches (36 centimeters) of snow. The storm system then entered Michigan, leaving another 14 inches (36 centimeters) of snow behind.

In January 1982, more blizzards struck these two states and Wisconsin. The storm disrupted the dairy industry in Wisconsin, making it impossible for milk to be delivered. The weekend of January 10 brought what was called the "Arctic outbreak of the century."

Temperatures plunged in many parts of the country. One billion dollars' worth of oranges and grapefruit were ruined in Florida. And on January 11, Augusta, Georgia, recorded an all-time low of 1°F (-17°C). Across the nation 120 people lost their lives during this one frigid weekend.

△ **27**

C H A P T E R **3**

# *Eastern Blizzards*

Even though most blizzards strike the midsection of the country, blizzards are by no means restricted to that area. The Eastern Seaboard has had its share of devastating snowstorms throughout the years. Sometimes these storms have been more dangerous than those in the Midwest simply because people in the East are not as prepared for them. This is especially true of the southern states. Towns and municipalities in states like South Dakota in the Midwest, and Maine in the Northeast, can dig themselves out after a blizzard much more quickly than states like the Carolinas, for example, which are not used to heavy snows. Often, southern

*Opposite:*
Many New Yorkers, like this one gliding through Times Square, strapped on skis to get around the city during the March 1993 blizzard.

*Opposite:*
This view of downtown
Manhattan, looking toward
Wall Street, shows downed
telephone and power lines
caused by The Blizzard
of '88.

states do not have the proper snow-removal equipment, or the work force to handle blizzards. And because of the rarity of snowstorms there, people are usually taken by surprise when a severe snowstorm hits.

Since the eastern part of the country was settled first, there are much earlier records of blizzards occurring in that area than farther west. These records date all the way back to the seventeenth century. The era of "modern-day" blizzards, however, begins at the end of the nineteenth century with The Blizzard of '88, the most well-documented storm in the history of North America.

## New York City: 1888

The forecast for New York City on March 11, 1888, was "cloudy followed by light rain and clearing." But what started as rain that Sunday evening soon turned to sleet and then snow— almost 2 feet (1 meter) of it. The temperature, springlike only 24 hours earlier, had dropped drastically. By early Monday, the blizzard had begun in earnest. Conscientious New Yorkers, not wanting to lose a day's wages, braved the blinding snow and high winds—and lived to regret it. The city's four elevated railroads all ground to a halt when the tracks iced over. Men that were on the ground put up tall ladders

# BLIZZARDS IN THE EARLY DAYS OF AMERICA

There are records of blizzards that go back to colonial times. One of the earliest eastern storms that we know about occurred during "The Terriblest Winter" of 1698. According to one journal writer in Dover, New Hampshire, it snowed for seventeen days straight. A later blizzard, "The Great Snow of 1717," consisted of four separate snowstorms that struck southern New England and left up to 5 feet (2 meters) of snow, and drifts as high as 25 feet (8 meters). "The Great Snow" was so notorious that historians called it by this name for over a century.

The most famous blizzard of the Revolutionary War period was "The Hessian Storm," which struck from Pennsylvania to New England on the day after Christmas in 1778. It was named for the Hessians—German soldiers who were hired to fight for the British. These soldiers were trapped in Rhode Island by snowdrifts that were up to 17 feet (5 meters) high.

and charged trapped passengers two dollars each to rescue them.

Other rescues were even more dramatic. A parish priest returning from a sick call noticed a hand sticking out of a snowdrift. It turned out to be the hand of one of his Sunday school students who had been sent out for food by his family. Some who were caught in the storm weren't found in time to be saved. One man froze to death trying to walk the single block from his job to his home. A woman staying with a friend on 96th Street saw a man try to cross the intersection in the wind and snow. "We watched him start, get quarter way across and then flung back against the building on the corner," she later wrote. "The last time he tried it, he was caught up in a whirl of snow and disappeared from our view. The next morning seven horses, policemen and his brother, charged [rammed] the drift and his body was *kicked* out of the drift."

Other people had the good sense to stay put. Women employed at Macy's department store were allowed to camp out overnight on cots in the furniture department. Ironically, March 12 was to be the "Spring Open Day" sale at Macy's and other stores throughout the city.

Monday night most theaters in the city were closed, although many saloons did a booming

△ **33**

A young woman stands in front of a tunnel that was sculpted through a snowdrift at Miss Porter's School in Farmington, Connecticut, after The Blizzard of '88.

business for those who could get to them. The circus at Madison Square Garden went on as scheduled with only a hundred brave souls attending. "If only one customer had come, I would have given the complete show," bragged circus owner P.T. Barnum.

By Tuesday morning, the storm was beginning to subside, but getting around town was still extremely difficult. Many homeowners dug tunnels from their doors to the street.  Signs on towering snowbanks showed that New Yorkers hadn't lost their sense of humor in the disaster. "Keep off the Grass" warned one sign.  Another read, "Don't pick the flowers."  A total of 21 inches (53 centimeters) of snow fell in New York City.  Much higher amounts were recorded upstate—31 inches (79 centimeters) in Albany, and 55 inches (140 centimeters) in Troy.  While most of the snow in New York City was gone in a few weeks, some patches remained in shady spots until June.

Meanwhile, in New England, many people, particularly the young, were having the time of their lives in the storm's aftermath.  One boy, thirteen-year-old William N. Beebe of Canaan, Connecticut, later wrote of his experience: "...there was a drift...which was 20 feet [6 meters] high and we kids dug channels all through it and from the center up through the top—and did we have fun pushing each other down through and falling into the soft snow at the bottom!  Then we would crawl out of one of the channels and repeat the performance."

By Thursday, New York City was almost back to normal, but the blizzard had taken its toll. Nearly 100 people were lost at sea in the nearby coastal waters of the Atlantic during the storm. Approximately 200 ships were wrecked or had disappeared.  A total of 800 people, more than 200 of those in New York City, perished in the storm system that stretched along the Eastern Coast from Maryland to Maine.  New York City alone suffered $20 million in property damage, including the destruction of homes, office buildings, and telegraph and telephone lines.

Perhaps one of the best descriptions of The Blizzard of '88 came from a news reporter who worked for Vermont's *Bellows Falls Times* and wrote: "No paths, no streets, no sidewalks, no lights, no roads, no guests, no calls, no teams, no hacks, no trains, no moon, no meat, no milk, no paper, no mail, no news, no thing— but snow."

## Washington, D.C.: 1922

"The Knickerbocker Storm" of January 27–29, 1922 dumped 28 inches (71 centimeters) of snow on Washington, D.C.  In the midst of the storm, a number of residents had gone to see a silent movie at the Knickerbocker Theater.  During the movie, 2 feet (1 meter) of snow that was on the roof caused the entire ceiling to collapse on the people below.  Plaster and debris rained down on top of the audience.  A chunk of cement crashed into the orchestra pit, instantly killing the bandleader and many of the musicians.  A woman in the neighborhood was alerted that something terrible had happened by a strange man pounding on her door. Since he spoke in Italian, she couldn't understand him, but she knew he was frightened. The man ran away and, without thinking, the woman ran into the street and pulled the fire alarm.

The hose truck of Engine Company 21 was the first to reach the theater. Firefighters found a huge pile of debris inside the Knickerbocker Theater with 18 inches (46 centimeters) of

Firemen and soldiers help clear the wreckage from the Knickerbocker Theater after the 1922 blizzard caused its roof to collapse.

cement piled on top. Suddenly someone shouted, "Here's a hand! Help me dig it out!" It quickly became clear that additional help would be needed.

The U.S. Marines and the U.S. Navy arrived to help with the rescue effort, which continued into the following night. Ninety-eight people perished in the theater, but the storm, which had moved from South Carolina to Massachusetts, had caused additional deaths—140 in all.

## Buffalo, New York: 1977

If the East has a "blizzard city" it would have to be Buffalo, New York, which sits next to cold, windy Lake Erie. Buffalo averages about 8 feet (2 meters) of snow annually. But the storm that struck on January 28, 1977, was bad, even by Buffalo standards. There were already 35 inches (89 centimeters) of snow covering the city when this fresh storm started. Blinding snow and winds up to 70 miles (113 kilometers) per hour trapped 17,000 people in downtown offices. Thousands of motorists were stranded in snowdrifts up to 30 feet (9 meters) high and had to be rescued by volunteers in snowmobiles. Snowmobiles were also used to transport food, blankets, and medicine to people stuck in whatever shelter they could find when the storm hit. The blizzard lasted for five straight days. City officials imposed a week-long ban on all travel, except during an emergency, so that snowplows could be used to properly clear the roads.

A total of nearly 1,000 National Guard members, marines, and army personnel helped to remove the seemingly endless mounds of snow. Many flew rescue missions, carrying fuel and food to snowbound farms in the nine adjoining counties that, along with Buffalo, were declared the first national disaster area in U.S. history. Since then, the federal government has come to the aid of many communities that have been struck by major natural disasters.

Despite the efforts of all involved, 23 people perished in the Buffalo blizzard, 9 of whom froze to death in their cars.

## Boston and New York City: 1977–1978

The winter of 1977-1978 was a tough one in the eastern United States. In many of the eastern states, snow and ice were a common sight for weeks on end. Much beachfront property was destroyed by strong winds and waves brought by winter storms. Particularly hard hit were New York City, and Boston, Massachusetts.

Boston streets were covered with 27 inches (69 centimeters) of snow during the blizzard of 1978 and some people actually got around on cross-country skis. On one of the main highways leading out of the city, more than 3,000 vehicles were left sitting on the road for four days, unable to move, and 75,000 people were without power when a roof caved in on a major generator. In February, 10,000 National Guard and army members were called in to aid in the rescue and snow removal efforts. The damage to property was in the millions, and 29 deaths occurred throughout Massachusetts.

Areas around New York City were under almost 18 inches (46 centimeters) of snow in 1978—a delight for children. Eleven-year-old Ricky Sanchez built an igloo at the edge of Van

U.S. Army bulldozers work to clear the streets of Boston after the 1978 blizzard. Road conditions were so bad that the city put a ban on driving for 24 hours so that the streets could be cleared.

This woman attached a sign to her car to keep snowplows from running into it.

Cortlandt Park. After hours of hard work he hollered boldly to a passerby: "Hey! Watch this while I run for a sandwich." Other kids banded together for snowball fights and sled racing. When the sun went down, they waited eagerly for the next day to play. "...I was back out before the sun was up today," one child told a reporter.

But for adults who had to get to work, the blizzard was a headache. New York had had its share of blizzards in the past; however, this storm went on record as one of the city's worst. On February 6, three commuter trains got stuck on Long Island. A diesel train evacuated 800 passengers after nearly nine hours. That train also got caught in the snow and another diesel ended up pushing it. The entire trip took close to twelve hours to complete. By February 8, the Long Island Railroad had no electric-powered trains running. The few diesel-powered trains that were operating were extremely delayed.

## The Storm of the Century: 1993

On March 11, 1993, exactly 105 years after The Blizzard of 1888, a monster snowstorm formed in the Gulf of Mexico. On Friday, March 12, it hit Florida and then moved northward, striking other eastern states and Canada's Maritime Provinces. It also hit parts of Cuba.

During the twentieth century, a number of other storms had dumped more snow on the area, were responsible for more deaths, and recorded higher winds than The Blizzard of '93. However, it has been labeled the "Storm of the Century" because of its great intensity and the extensive area it affected. On the day after the storm struck the metropolitan area, a reporter for *The New York Times* called it "a monster with the heart of a blizzard and the soul of a hurricane."

Hurricane-force winds reached 109 miles (175 kilometers) per hour in Franklin County, Florida. Florida was also hit by more than 50 tornadoes, affecting Homestead, an area that had already been devastated by Hurricane Andrew in the previous year. Record-low temperatures were reported in the usually warm southern states.

A line of snowplows works its way from Washington, D.C., towards Arlington, Virginia, as snow continues to fall. The Lincoln Memorial building is in the background.

△ **43**

The Storm of the Century resulted in the closing of many airports along the Eastern Seaboard. Here, a Continental jet is snowbound at LaGuardia Airport in New York.

"We don't have the clothes or the winter survival kits like people up North," said Weather Service officer Wayne Jones in Greer, South Carolina. "If someone is caught outside, this is not survivable." These words proved all too true when one man froze to death in Birmingham, Alabama, where temperatures hit a low of 2°F (-17°C). The highest amounts of snowfall recorded were 50 inches (127 centimeters) at Mount Mitchell, North Carolina, and 36 inches (91 centimeters) at Syracuse, New York.

The death toll from The Blizzard of '93 was 238, but this figure does not include 48 sailors who were missing from vessels that sank off Nova Scotia, Canada, and in the Gulf of Mexico.

The greatest number of U.S. deaths was in Pennsylvania, where 50 people lost their lives, and in Florida, where the death toll was 44. Canada reported 4 deaths, and Cuba reported 3.

Financially, the Storm of the Century cost the United States hundreds of millions of dollars. In New York, for example, expenses for the snow removal alone were about $16 million. At the storm's height, more than 3 million people lost electrical power, thousands were forced to leave their homes as a result of coastal flooding, and travelers were stranded when airports and highways closed.

Some people refused to allow the storm to ruin their plans. One woman in Westchester County, New York, decided to go ahead with her wedding, despite the swirling snow. "I have some white boots," she told a reporter. "...I'll wear those to the church and carry my heels. Everyone's saying this is a day I will truly never forget."

Other people found things to celebrate, too. A hardware store owner in Simpsonville, South Carolina, was happy to report, "I sold out of the 20 to 30 sleds I had been stuck with for two years." A man in Washington, D.C., turned his sailboat into a sail ski and raced it across the capital's Mall, where about 14 inches (36 centimeters) of snow had fallen on March 13.

△ **45**

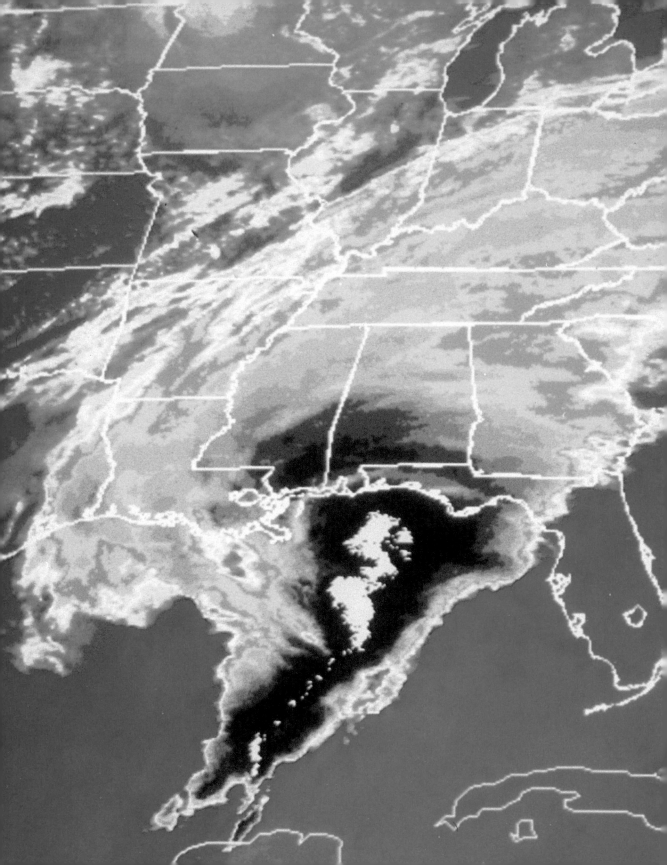

CHAPTER

# *Blizzard Preparation and Protection*

Being prepared for a blizzard when it strikes is critical to saving lives and property, and minimizing damage.  If people don't know where and when a blizzard is going to hit, they can't be prepared for it.

Technology and science have dramatically improved the forecasting of snowstorms in recent years.  Meteorologists, scientists who specialize in analyzing weather data, often use weather satellites orbiting in space to photograph the earth with television cameras.  Picture signals are beamed from the satellite to weather stations on the ground.  Photographs are then

*Opposite:*
Satellite pictures can illustrate storm conditions. The various colors indicate how high and how cold the storm clouds are.

processed from these signals. The photographs can show cloud masses, out of which storm systems develop. Meteorologists look at the satellite photographs and spot blizzards and other storms forming over the oceans. By observing the movement of clouds in a series of satellite photographs, meteorologists can also determine fairly well the direction a storm is moving in and its speed. They can then pinpoint a storm's exact location using radar. The radar signals bounce off ice and snow in the atmosphere.

In addition, the National Weather Service receives weather observations from hundreds of local weather stations throughout the country. This data helps them to predict just where and when a storm will pass over a particular state or region, and what conditions residents there can expect.

Of course, due to a certain number of variables, storm predictions aren't always foolproof. Weather conditions can change rapidly, sometimes making it impossible to say exactly what will happen next. A lack of observation systems that can thoroughly cover the entire span of the oceans is another factor that may lead to inaccurate predictions. Satellites alone cannot provide enough detailed information about the atmosphere over these vast areas of water. This lack of data hampers meteorologists' ability to track storms that develop offshore.

## *Storm Watches and Warnings*

After gathering whatever information it can, the National Weather Service makes its forecast for each part of the country and sends out weather reports to newspapers, and radio and television stations. It also sends reports to airports, where accurate weather readings are of the utmost importance to pilots and passengers.

National Weather Service meteorologists analyze and discuss extensive data so that they are able to issue storm warnings when necessary.

When a blizzard is headed for a certain area, the National Weather Service will issue a storm watch. This watch alerts residents that a snowstorm is approaching their area. The storm may change its course before striking, so people are

## ON THE ROAD IN A BLIZZARD

Nobody wants to be stuck in a motor vehicle during a blizzard. But sometimes people have to go out in the storm for a good reason. Here are some tips to keep in mind before you get into a car or truck with an older friend or family member:

- Plan your route carefully. Know where you're going and how to get there. You don't want to get lost in a blizzard.
- Make sure the vehicle is ready. Check the gas tank; be sure you have enough gas to get where you are going. Make sure there is plenty of antifreeze in the radiator. Keep a sack of sand in the trunk in case you need it. Don't go out unless your vehicle has snow tires or chains. Also carry a flashlight, emergency flares, a spare tire, and other emergency supplies.

If the vehicle you are riding in does get stuck, follow these steps:

- Stay put. Your first reaction may be to leave the vehicle to look for shelter. But you can easily lose your way and could freeze to death. It's safer to stay in the vehicle and keep warm. It will also be easier for rescuers to find you.
- Make a flag. Run up the antenna on the vehicle and tie a piece of brightly colored material to it to signal passersby.
- Keep windows opened slightly if you run the motor. Each year a number of people die of carbon monoxide poisoning in vehicles stuck in blizzards. If you let the motor run to stay warm, *never* keep the windows entirely shut. Fresh air entering the vehicle will prevent you from suffocating and keep you awake and alert.
- Keep your body moving. Even though you're sitting in the vehicle, it's important that you move your body every so often to keep your blood circulating. This will prevent your limbs from freezing or developing frostbite. Movement will also give off body heat and keep you warmer. Clap your hands, shake your arms, and stamp your feet regularly.

told to tune in for further developments. If the storm continues on its path and draws nearer, the Weather Service next issues a storm warning. A warning tells residents that the storm or blizzard will soon strike their community and that they should take immediate measures to protect their family and property. Three kinds of snowstorm warnings the National Weather Service issues are:

**Heavy storm warning**—snowfall of 4 inches (10 centimeters) or more is expected within 12 hours, or 6 inches (15 centimeters) within 24 hours.

**Blizzard warning**—heavy snowfall blown by winds of at least 35 miles (56 kilometers) per hour is expected.

**Severe blizzard warning**—heavy snowfall blown by winds of at least 45 miles (72 kilometers) per hour is expected, accompanied by temperatures of 10°F (-12°C) or lower.

## How Towns and Cities Get Ready

Once a blizzard warning has been issued, cities and towns get their snowplows and other road equipment ready to roll. Employees who run the machinery prepare to go out as soon as the storm starts. Town employees check roadside drums and boxes to make sure they are filled with a mixture of sand and salt. If stuck in the snow, a motorist can throw some of the mixture under the car's tires for traction.

Plows shovel fallen snow off roadways, trying to keep an accumulation from building up. Trucks scatter sand on road surfaces to keep motor vehicles from skidding. Salt spreaders are used to melt snow on highways and local streets. Once the storm strikes, road crews may be out for hours. It is very challenging work for the snowplow drivers. "You've got to think of safety," said Frank Gallo of New York City, cleaning up after the Storm of the Century. "That's the main thing on this job. If you hit a sewer cap, you can rip that plow right off. It gets to you. It gets a little lonely. You sing to yourself, you talk to yourself."

Keeping roads open during a blizzard is extremely important. Most people will stay in their homes, but emergency vehicles, including fire trucks and ambulances, must be able to get out and about; people's lives depend on it.

### How Residents Prepare and Protect Themselves

While town and municipal employees make preparations for clearing the roads, residents must also get ready for an impending blizzard. People in rural areas nail sheets of tar paper around the bottom of their homes and pile branches against the tar paper.  When winds blow snow against the house, drifts form that insulate the house from the cold air.  Farmers cover machinery and tractors.  Livestock and other animals are brought into warm barns for the duration of the storm.

To ensure that you will be well prepared in the event a blizzard strikes your area, you should keep a checklist of things you need to do:

• Fill bathtubs with water.  If you don't have water during the storm because your pipes have frozen, you will have fresh water for drinking, cooking, and flushing.

• Secure your property.  Make sure all windows and doors are tightly closed and that anything movable in the yard is tied down or brought inside.  Bring pets indoors, too!

• Stock up.  Before the storm comes, get to the market to buy food supplies, especially food that doesn't require cooking.  Also get extra batteries for radios and flashlights.  People taking prescription medication should call their doctors and arrange to have an ample supply on hand.

• Stay inside.  Once the storm hits, don't go outside unless it's absolutely necessary.  The blinding snow can bring visibility down to zero, and you could get lost within a few yards of your home.

If you must go out in the snow in order to accompany a family member, or in an emergency situation, keep the following in mind.

- Dress warmly.  Put on several layers of clothing to insulate your body, and don't forget gloves and a hat.
- Don't overtire yourself.  Just walking in heavy snow is strenuous; shoveling snow or pushing a car can be exhausting.
- Stay away from downed wires.  You could be burned or electrocuted by overhead wires that have fallen.  If you can, report any downed wires to power-company employees to investigate and repair; that's their job.

## Cleaning Up

After the blizzard passes, there is the enormous job of removing all that snow.  Snowplows go into full gear to push snow off streets and highways.  Sometimes this can be a difficult task.  Freezing temperatures can make the fallen snow rock-hard.  Rubber-tipped snowplows can be wrecked and become useless, as happened in parts of New England following The Blizzard of '93.  Stronger, tougher plows must be used, or the snow will be impossible to remove until warmer temperatures soften it.

After the snow is plowed into tall mountains on street corners, it must often be moved again.

△ **55**

Many cities use special dump trucks with buckets attached to conveyor belts that scoop up the snow and drop it into the trucks. Then the snow is likely to be dumped into water—a river, lake, or ocean—where it melts.

In some areas, such as in Colorado's Rocky Mountains, dump trucks are too slow. There, a kind of plow called a snowblast is used. A snowblast has a huge paddle wheel in front that

A front-end loader dumps a bucket of snow into a vat of warm water during the cleanup of The Blizzard of '93.

## BLIZZARD HEALTH HAZARDS

You're out in a blizzard, and it's freezing cold. You know you shouldn't be outside, but the storm caught you by surprise. You start to feel a strange tingling sensation in your ears, nose, hands, and feet. It's time to get inside, where it's warm, as fast as you can. You are experiencing the first signs of frostbite, damage to the skin and underlying tissues caused by below-freezing temperatures.

If you ignore the first signs of frostbite, your exposed body parts can become numb. If only the skin and underlying tissues are damaged, recovery may be complete. However, if blood vessels are affected, the tissues will die. This tissue death is called gangrene. If gangrene sets in, it may even be necessary to amputate the affected body parts before the damage spreads to the rest of the body.

The best treatment for a patient who has frostbite is to place the affected body parts in warm, not hot, water. This will slowly restore circulation and warmth to the skin and tissue.

Another condition that can result from exposure to blizzard conditions is called hypothermia. In hypothermia, the victim's body temperature drops below 95°F (35°C), which results in slowing down the heartbeat and the flow of blood. In severe hypothermia, especially if the body temperature falls below 90°F (32°C), the person may die as bodily functions begin to shut down.

The treatment for hypothermia is similar to that for frostbite. The victim is placed in a warm bath and is later wrapped up in warm blankets. A physician should be notified at the first sign of hypothermia.

cuts through snowdrifts like butter. In the back of the machine is a jet blower that sprays out the snow in a 30-foot (9-meter) arc into canyons or gullies. A snowblast can clear snow off a road or an airport runway with amazing speed and efficiency.

Cleaning up after a blizzard can be costly. In regions where snowfall tends to be heavy, towns and cities set aside money in a special budget for snow removal. If they go through it

Cleaning up after a blizzard can be an enormous task. This man is digging out his car in Squaw Valley, California.

before winter ends, money must be taken from other parts of the municipal budget.

Good or bad, blizzards are a part of life in much of North America. They are also among the most awesome of nature's disasters. Unlike tornadoes, hurricanes, and earthquakes, blizzards have a truly beautiful side that sometimes makes us forget their terrible power. If we respect the power of these fierce snowstorms and are aware of their dangers, we can safely enjoy and appreciate their magical wonders.

# *Glossary*

**air mass**  A large body of air in which the temperature, humidity, and air pressure are about the same throughout.

**blizzard**  A heavy snowstorm with very cold temperatures, sustained winds of 35 miles (56 kilometers) per hour, and visibility of less than 0.25 miles (0.4 kilometers).

**blizzard warning**  A warning issued by the National Weather Service that tells residents a heavy snowfall blown by winds of at least 35 miles (56 kilometers) per hour is expected.

**cold front**  A boundary between a cold air mass and a warmer air mass, caused by the cold air mass pushing the warmer air mass out of the way.

**frostbite**  An injury to the skin that is caused by exposure to extreme cold.

**gangrene**  The death of body tissue, usually caused by a loss of blood supply.

**heavy storm warning**  A warning issued by the National Weather Service that tells residents to expect a snowfall of 4 inches (10 centimeters) or more within 12 hours, or 6 inches (15 centimeters) or more within 24 hours.

**hypothermia** A drop in body temperature below 95°F (35°C) resulting from exposure to extreme cold, which causes the heart and breathing rates to slow down.

**meteorologist** A scientist who specializes in analyzing weather data.

**National Weather Service** A federal agency, headquartered in Washington, D.C., that provides weather forecasts and observations, and maintains weather records for the United States.

**severe blizzard warning** A warning issued by the National Weather Service, informing residents that a heavy snowfall blown by winds of at least 45 miles (72 kilometers) per hour, accompanied by temperatures of 10°F (-12°C) or lower, is expected.

**snowblast** A snowplow that quickly cuts through snow with a huge paddle wheel and blows it out in a 30-foot (9-meter) arc into canyons or gullies.

**snow fence** A fence set up along roadways that traps falling snow and prevents it from drifting onto roads.

**storm watch** A notice issued by the National Weather Service that alerts residents that a snowstorm is approaching and may strike in the immediate future.

# *Further Reading*

Bentley, W.A. and Humphreys, W.J. *Snow Crystals*. Magnolia, MA: Peter Smith, 1962.

Caplovich, Judd. *Blizzard! The Great Storm of '88*. Vernon, CT: Vero Publishing, 1987.

Fradin, Dennis Brindell. *Blizzards and Winter Weather*. Chicago, IL: Childrens Press, 1983.

Knapp, Brian. *Storm*. Madison, NJ: Raintree Steck-Vaughn, 1990.

Lampton, Christopher. *Blizzard*. Brookfield, CT: Millbrook Press, 1991.

Steele, Philip. *Snow: Causes and Effects*. New York: Watts, 1991.

Stonehouse, Bernard. *Snow, Ice, and Cold*. New York: Macmillan, 1992.

Williams, Terry T. and Major, Ted. *The Secret Language of Snow*. New York: Pantheon, 1984.

## HAVE YOU EVER FACED A DISASTER?

If you have ever had to be brave enough to face a blizzard, you probably have a few exciting stories to tell! Twenty-First Century Books invites you to write us a letter and share your experiences. The letter can describe any aspect of your true story—how you felt during the disaster; what happened to you, your family, or other people in your area; or how the disaster changed your life. Please send your letter to Disaster Editor, TFCB, 115 West 18th Street, New York, NY 10011. We look forward to hearing from you!

# *Source Notes*

"Blizzard Conditions." *Time*, March 22, 1993.

"The Blizzard of '93." *Newsweek*, March 22, 1993.

Brandt, Nat. *The Great Blizzard of '88.* American Heritage, 1977.

Brown, Walter R., and Anderson, Norman D. *Historical Catastrophes: Snowstorms and Avalanches.* Reading, MA: Addison-Wesley, 1976.

Caplovich, Judd. *Blizzard! The Great Storm of '88.* Vernon, CT: Vero Publishing, 1987.

Evans, Eva Knox. *The Snow Book.* Boston, MA: Little, Brown & Co., 1965.

Whipple, A.B.C. *Storm.* New York: Time-Life Books, 1982.

# Index

America's breadbasket, 15
Aspen, Colorado, 15

Barnum, P. T., 34
Beebe, William N., 35
Bentley, Wilson "Snowflake", 9
Blizzard of 1888, 42
    in New York City, 30, 33–36
    in South Dakota, 21
Blizzard of 1905, 21
Blizzard of '93, 42–45, 55 *See also* The
    Storm of the Century.
Blizzard country, 17, 18, 22
Blizzard state. *See* South Dakota.
Blizzards
    benefits of, 13, 15
    cleaning up after, 55–57
    dangers of, 8, 10, 12–13
    definition of, 6–7
    health hazards of, 57
    preparing for, 51–55
    trapped in vehicles during, 50
Blizzards of 1966, The, 25, 27
Blizzards of 1981–1982, The, 27
Boston, Massachusetts, 39–40
Buffalo, New York, 38–39

Canaan, Connecticut, 35
Cold fronts, 8

Dalton, Georgia, 6
Dog sleds, 18
Donner Party, 20
Donner Pass, 20

Eastern Seaboard, 5, 6, 29
    blizzards on, 29–45

Farmers (and blizzards), 10, 12, 18
Frostbite, 57

Gallo, Frank, 52
Gangrene, 57
Great Blizzard of 1949, The, 22–25
"Great White Death", 24 *See also* The
    Great Blizzard of 1949.
Gulf of Mexico, 5, 42, 44

Higgenbotham, Jeff, 6
Hurricane Andrew, 43
Hypothermia, 57

Jericho, Vermont, 9
Jones, Wayne, 44

Knickerbocker Storm, The, 36–38
Knickerbocker Theater, 36, 37

Macy's department store, 33
Madison Square Garden, 34
McNay, Colonel Joe, 24
Meteorologists, 47, 48
Missouri River, 20

National Guard, 39, 40
National Weather Service, 6–7, 44, 48,
    49–50, 51
New York City, 30, 35, 36, 39, 40
Northern Plains, 15, 22

Offutt Air Base, 24
Operation Snowbound, 23, 24

Pick, General Lewis A., 24

Quebec, Canada, 6

Reed, J.F., 20
Reed, Virginia, 20
Rockport, Colorado, 24

Salt spreaders, 52
Sanchez, Ricky, 40–41
Sierra Nevada Mountains, 20
Ski planes, 18
Snowblast, 56–57

*Snow Crystals*, 9
Snow fences, 17–18
Snowmobiles, 18
Snowplows, 51, 52, 55
Snow shoes, 18
South Dakota (and blizzards), 19–21
Squaw Valley, California, 15
Storm of the Century, The, 5, 42–45, 52
Storm watches and warnings, 49–51
Stowe, Vermont, 15

Vail, Colorado, 15

Washington, D.C., 6, 36, 45
Weather satellites, 47–48

**Acknowledgements and Photo Credits**

Cover: ©Evan Agostini/Gamma-Liaison; p. 4: ©Alan Weiner/Gamma-Liaison; p. 9: ©1992 Scott Camazine/Photo Researchers, Inc.; pp. 11, 12, 22, 26, 37: UPI/Bettmann; pp. 14, 16, 19: South Dakota Tourism; pp. 15, 58: Sacramento Bee/Randy Pench/Gamma-Liaison; pp. 23, 43, 44, 54, 56: Wide World Photos; p. 28: Levy/Gamma-Liaison; pp. 31, 32: The Bettmann Archive; p. 34: The New-York Historical Society; pp. 40, 41, 49: AP/Wide World Photos; p. 46: The National Oceanic and Atmospheric Administration.